Trams Hill Howth

A photographic tribute

...ames Kilroy

I wish to dedicate this book to all those people worldwide who work tirelessly to restore trams, record their history, lecture or write on them, or simply talk about them over a pint. These people are my friends.

Photograph by Mia Kilroy

Jim Kilroy was born in the village of Artane in 1943. He attended the Christian Brothers School at Marino until 1955, and completed his education with the Marist Fathers in Dundalk, Co Louth. He chose architecture as his profession and qualified in 1968 from University College Dublin. A year later he married his wife Helen and had two daughters, Claire and Mia. Jim has fond memories of the Dublin Trams and joined the Transport Museum Society in 1976, where he is now the Director of Tram Restoration. He is a keen horseman and represented Howth Riding Club at the RDS on four occasions. As an architect he is involved with urban renewal and his special interest is refurbishment of old buildings and street and in-fill design. This is his third book on trams; the other two were *Howth and Her Trams* and *Irish Trams*.

6 5 4 3 2 1

©James Kilroy
Newtownards 1998

Designed by Colourpoint Books,
Newtownards
Maps drawn by James Kilroy
Printed by ColourBooks

ISBN 1 898392 13 7

Colourpoint Books
Unit D5, Ards Business Centre
Jubilee Road
NEWTOWNARDS
County Down
Northern Ireland
BT23 4YH
Tel: (01247) 820505/819787 Ex 239
Fax: (01247) 821900
E-mail: info@colourpoint.co.uk
Web-site: www.colourpoint.co.uk

Unless otherwise stated, the photographs in this book are from the James Kilroy & Brian Greene collections.

Cover photograph: Hill of Howth tram No 6 loading passengers at Sutton railway station. It must have been some ladies' outing – note the two ladies in navy coats with red bands on their hats. The noonday sun sends piercing shadows across the forecourt and the traction column and outreach strikingly cast their image down the upper dash and windscreen.   *R L Ludgate*

Frontispiece: Every number of years, the IRRS and the LRTL got together to sample some railway oddity at risk of closure in Ireland. Here we see a full tram load with No 9 at Sutton sheds on 7 June 1958. Side by side in the centre of the photograph we see Billy Rankin (conductor) and a very proud Christy Hanway (motorman) with his hands clasped.
Courtesy National Tramway Museum, Crich

Rear cover photograph: Lia Ludgate (wife of the late R L Ludgate) beside the sign at Howth station which directed passengers to the trams.   *R L Ludgate*

CONTENTS

Thank You

I would like to give a special thanks to all those many people who have encouraged and supported me in my endeavours over the years, too many to mention. I cannot however omit to mention just a few who stand out. Bernard McQuillan of McQuillan Tools, who has provided me with free tools over many years. Ian Lenni and all at HGW who have given paint without charge since the beginning, and Michael Chadwick of Chadwicks for all the ply and glue. Thanks also to Don Bailey for abrasives and fillers, Willy Hendy of Ferrum Trading and Denis Kane of Reynolds Systems. Tuck Fasteners have always given me a good deal on nuts and bolts. Judy Fegan deserves thanks for her advice and support, Colm and Oisin for being there for me always, and also Jack Kinane and Jimmy and Vera McDonnagh for minding the pennies. Without their constant help and support to a small volunteer group, progress would have been nigh impossible.

A special thanks to Michael and Aileen Pollard for their assistance with proof reading the book and to John Gillham for permission to use his excellent map of the Hill of Howth Tramway.

Introduction

The first trams I remember were those from Dublin city, operated by the Dublin United Tramways Company (DUT) and, in their final years of running, by Coras Iompair Eireann (CIE), the Irish Transport Company. My father was a reporter for the *Irish Press* at the time and he had the privilege of recording the final moments of these graceful and powerful machines. My memory of them was of their enormous size compared with their puny metallic cousins, the motor buses, which, at the time, were poised to replace them. The Dublin trams were massive green and cream cars, covered with panels of advertisements and they travelled in close proximity to one another along busy streets carrying throngs of Dubliners going about their business. On their last operating day, 9 July 1949, crowds of onlookers filled the streets, many singing and shouting in a jovial manner, others silent with a sense of pending doom, as these fine vehicles made tracks into history.

The Hill of Howth trams were very different indeed. To begin with, they were much older trams, built in 1901 and 1902, and were of the open-top bogie variety. Instead of busy city streets they wound their circuitous way through seascapes and hills. Busy throngs of workers were replaced by happy holiday crowds on an adventure through the scenic peninsula. Unlike their city counterparts, they seldom carried advertisements and their livery was Oxford blue and cream lined out with gold and had large red lettering and colourful monograms. They had a cheerful exciting appearance as they glided along through rocky outcrops and by fields of corn.

Howth

At the start of the 19th century, the peninsula of Howth was very sparsely populated and, apart from the lord in his castle at Howth demesne, the village of fearless fishermen and a few wealthy refugees from the city, the landscape looked untouched and primeval. The Hill was studded with history from stone age dolmens, celtic forts, and early Christian oratories, to Viking ramparts and Norman castles. Each episode left its distinct manifestations like a multitude of varied gemstones in a necklace of time. The trams seemed to unweave this history as they passed from the megalithic tombs of Sutton past the stone tower on Corr Hill to the royal cairns of Shielmartin Hill, by the saintly stones of St Fintan's 7th century oratory, the celtic fort of King Griffin at the Baily, before finally descending Howth Castle grounds with its prehistoric cromlach built over 4,000 years ago, rhododendron clad rocks and magnificent maritime views — and of course past the castle itself, which dates from the 13th century. Howth had a magic of its very own, and in some special way the trams unravelled the pages of history as each episode unfolded. The demise of the electric trams and their glorious journey through this magnificent and historic hill was a great loss and a cause of great sadness to the people of Dublin. The Edwardian daytrippers, who first came to explore the hill, found that the tramway had opened up pathways around a secluded and secret terrain untouched for centuries. The tram was a journey into the past, a voyage of discovery.

The silver rails serpentining their way through the undergrowth were almost invisible threads of transport and caused little disruption, whereas the large soul-less roadways that replaced them lie heavily across the face of the hill, defiling her sanctity and bringing a flood of cars and buses into the heart of this once peaceful land. The trams floated gently through its woods and dells in a manner that caused no disharmony. The combustion engine with all its noise and fumes could never have replaced the charm and serenity of these lovely electric cars.

Howth harbour was constructed in the early decades of the 19th century as part of a plan to improve the lines of travel and communication between London and Dublin. The GPO in London engaged the services of the world famous bridge and canal builder, Thomas Telford, to select a road and sea route to link the

In the first of three views, taken at the turn of the century, the Abbey of Howth stands dramatically on the edge of a cliff overlooking the harbour. The original church was founded by King Sitric, the Dane, in 1042. Almaric, Lord of Howth, gave it a grant of land and in 1235 the north aisle was added. The chantry was added by Christopher, the 13th Baron, in the early fifteenth century and the abbey is the burial place of the Lords of Howth. It was abandoned as a place of worship around 1645. The stone building on the left is the College of Howth.

J Kilroy collection

This view is taken at the lower end of Balglass Road, which becomes Balkill Road as it rises to the Summit. The tram would have crossed this road some short distance behind the photographer before serpentining its way down to Howth harbour, which can be seen to the extreme left. Balglass Road turns sharply right at the end of this view and almost immediately sharply left to become the 'main street' through Howth village, which can be seen to the right. The evenly tilled field is a pleasure to behold.

J Kilroy collection

respective capitals — after all Dublin, in those days, was the second city of the British Empire. To travel between London and Dublin in the early 1800s was a perilous and slow journey by coach, foot, horse and sailing boat, and could take two weeks. Lurking robbers and stormy seas claimed many a victim. Telford's new road and harbour plan was the largest road building project since the time of the Romans and passed over some of Telford's finest bridges. Telford initially selected Howth as the berth for the mailboat and the Howth to Dublin road via Raheny was all part of this courageous plan. However, in 1822 the mail boat berth was switched to Dun Laoghaire (then Kingstown) to the south of Dublin and this was a great loss to Howth. The move to Dun Laoghaire was reinforced by the construction of the Dublin and Kingstown Railway in 1834. Although the Dublin and Drogheda Railway built a branch line from Howth Junction to the peninsula of Howth in 1847 to serve the harbour, it was too late and the mail boat never returned.

The East Pier has remained a popular and bracing walk for energetic Dubliners since the opening of the Harbour in 1817. A tram can just be seen at the end of Abbey Street adjoining the right end of the white terrace.

James Kilroy collection

The arrival of the Dublin and Drogheda Railway would not have heralded the first railway in Howth. Certainly it was the first mainline passenger railway but industrial and contractor's railways existed long before this. A short history of the evolution of this type of railway is found in my book *Irish Trams*, so I won't go into any further detail here. It is highly likely that some form of railway was used during the construction of Howth Harbour, commencing in 1807. All contractors associated with large constructional

undertakings, would have had knowledge about the benefit of providing a 'smooth thoroughfare' over which the ballast wagons would have made easier passage. The tracks might not have been steel in the conventional sense, but laid as flat strips with outer upstands and these were known as 'plateways'. They would have been laid over a public road with relative ease and removed on completion of the project.

On Friday 10 June 1814, the first stone was laid for the Roman Catholic chapel at the town end of Church Road within the village. This was the first of many stones from Kilrock quarries which at the

The first Roman Catholic chapel at Howth (1814), showing the position of the low relief wagons depicted on the church wall.

James Kilroy

6

The granite wagon symbol on the wall of the 1814 Roman Catholic chapel, Howth, erected as an expression of gratitude to the labourers at Kilrock quarries.

James Kilroy

The rail cart used to transport stone slabs from Kilrock quarries to Howth harbour. This cart is now at the Transport Museum in Howth.

Bob Dawson

time was providing the filling stone for the new harbour now nearing completion. The foundations for the harbour were imported from Runcorn and the sides and top were of Wicklow granite. The local stone, not ideal for such construction work, was compressed and compacted in between. The Kilrock quarry labourers gave generously of their time in the construction of the church, using a temporary railway to bring the stone up Abbey Street to the church. Not only did they drop the stones but they also built the chapel. As a mark of gratitude for their generosity of spirit, the parish priest of the day, the Rev John Smith, commemorated their work by erecting two granite railway wagons, at first floor level, on either side of the entrance. These railway symbols are a source of great surprise to all passers-by. In terms of religious symbolism, the spoked wheel was the symbol of the sun god in ancient Celtic times and 'Spiritual Transport' was also a theme. There is a possibility that this is the only instance of an overt railway symbol adorning a church.

There were also some mining operations in both the west and east mountain areas, but it is more likely that these were serviced by crude roads and horse and cart haulage. Until very recently, narrow gauge railway tracks were used at the screening plant at Baltray, on the left hand side as one approaches Howth and small carts were used to distribute the excavated material over the site, part of which is now owned by the Tecrete concrete factory.

Jerry O'Brien, the last man to keep cattle on the east mountain, and who was known locally as 'king of the east mountain', died at 90 years of age in 1997. He ran Howth riding stables and his family have long associations with horses on the peninsula for many generations. During the 1880s a fierce storm broke up the west pier of Howth harbour and Jerry O'Brien said that his family were involved with the transporting of stone along a temporary railway down to the harbour. Instead of horses, donkeys were used and there is a field behind Nashville Terrace where the donkeys were kept, known locally as the 'ass's field'. By coincidence, I now keep donkeys in this field, but as pets, not beasts of burden. It was here that one of my donkeys, Sophie, was slain in a satanic ritual as part of a curse placed on a previous owner. A small mound of stone marks the spot.

Earlier this year when cleaning up a field in the possession of the Lynch family, a well known local family of solicitors, I came across some 15lb narrow gauge railway track. The owner told me that his grandfather picked it up at a good price around the turn of the century and they were used as uprights to fence in a tennis court. It is likely that these were the tracks used for the repair of the east pier. Incidentally those who walk the east pier will notice a kink, or elbow, midway along and this is where the pier broke away in the storms. A sample of this rail can be seen at our Howth Museum.

The Clontarf and Hill of Howth Tramroad

The 1890 tramway proposal

The first proposal for a tramway to Howth was as early as 1890, when a forerunner of the CHHT proposed a line primarily intended to serve the busy fishing harbour at Howth. This proposal was for a three foot, narrow gauge line to commence in Mary's Lane opposite the North City Markets, which was the main outlet for the fish trade in the city. The line would have descended Cape Street and then gone down Parnell Street and on to Ballybough via Summerhill Road, and eastwards to Fairview. The tramway would then have taken the inland route along the Howth Road, and through Raheny village, to regain the coastal road at Kilbarrack and on to Howth village. The route would have brought the trams close to the GNR line from Amiens Street through Howth Junction to Howth, and would have passed near the stations at Clontarf, Killester, Raheny and Kilbarrack. This 1890 proposal would have been operated by horse power. Although electric traction had already made its appearance at the Giant's Causeway in 1883 and on the Bessbrook to Newry Tramway two years later, it was still regarded as an experimental mode of haulage.

At the Howth end, the tramway would have terminated with a branch along the East Pier, passing right by the fishing fleet and crates of fish. It is to be assumed that the transportation of fish would have been by special early morning wagons, so that the smells would not offend passengers. Neither the narrow gauge nor the fish wagons ever featured in the eventual Dublin to Howth tramway. However, in the early years the trams did bring fish crates or boxes, loaded onto the leading platform, as far as Nelson's Pillar. Push carts then picked them up and continued the journey to the markets. This service, though very small in proportion to traffic, did however earn these trams the nickname of 'Fish Trams'.

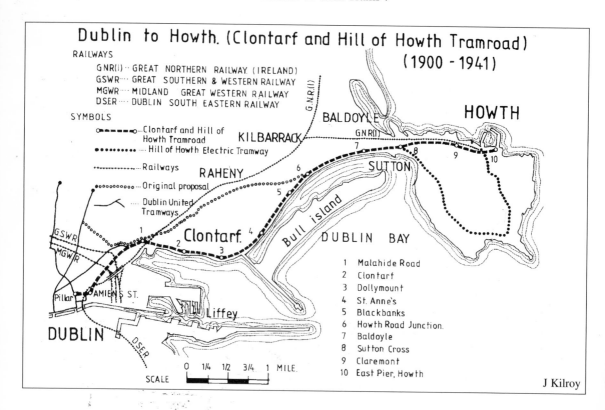

Dublin to Howth. (Clontarf and Hill of Howth Tramroad) (1900 - 1941)

RAILWAYS
GNR(I) ·· GREAT NORTHERN RAILWAY (IRELAND)
GSWR ··· GREAT SOUTHERN & WESTERN RAILWAY
MGWR ··· MIDLAND GREAT WESTERN RAILWAY
DSER ··· DUBLIN SOUTH EASTERN RAILWAY

SYMBOLS
— Clontarf and Hill of Howth Tramroad
··· Hill of Howth Electric Tramway
··· Railways
··· Original proposal
··· Dublin United Tramways

1 Malahide Road
2 Clontarf
3 Dollymount
4 St. Anne's
5 Blackbanks
6 Howth Road Junction
7 Baldoyle
8 Sutton Cross
9 Claremont
10 East Pier, Howth

SCALE 0 1/4 1/2 3/4 1 MILE

J Kilroy

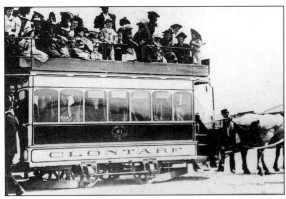

In 1873, the Dublin Tramways Co (1871-1881) provided a horse tramway to Dollymount. Seen here is car No 61, built in May 1884, setting off from Dollymount to the city with a tram packed with ladies. *Brian Greene collection*

Having just passed under the Skew Bridge carrying the GNR Railway to Belfast, Milnes car No 29 is nearing the tram sheds at Clontarf. The arch to the left now forms part of the roadway. *The Railway World, Jan 1898*

The Clontarf and Hill of Howth Tramroad

A new proposal, for a five foot three inch gauge tramway, was made on 20 Feb 1894, when the Clontarf and Hill of Howth Tramway Co (renamed the Clontarf and Hill of Howth Tramroad Co Ltd on 2 August 1898) proposed a line to commence at the Dublin United Tramways terminus at Dollymount (Clontarf) and proceed along the coastal route via 'Raheny-on-Strand' to Sutton and Howth. The CHHT further proposed to extend their tramway to the Hill of Howth. This extention would have risen from Claremont Gates, passed the GNR station at Howth at a high level and ascended more or less directly to the Summit. However, the concept was ill-considered as the gradients along the suggested route were in places as high as 1 in 18, which was too dangerous for horse traction and impossible for steam. At this date there were no electric trams in the Dublin area.

For two years nothing came of this plan, but in 1896 electric trams began to appear in Dublin, when the Dublin Southern Districts Tramways Co electrified its route into the City from Dalkey. The Dublin United Tramways Co (hitherto horse operated) formed a new company — the Dublin United Tramways Co (1896) Ltd — and amalgamated with the DSDT. (This amalgamation did not become legal, however, until 1905.) The DUT then began electrifying its own routes, and the first section to be energised was from Clontarf Depot to Annesley Bridge on 11 November 1897, with electric trams running through to Nelson's Pillar in

In Jan 1898, *The Railway World* carried a feature on the newly opened electric line from Dollymount to Nelson's Pillar, extolling its virtues. Here we see the tram depot at Dollymount. The double tracks continue on to the terminus, approximately three quarters of a mile further on towards Howth. This building is now a *Dublin Bus* depot. The tram fleet was supplied by Milnes of Birkenhead.

The Railway World

O'Connell Street on 19 March 1898. The arrival of electric traction led the CHHT to recommend its use on their proposed tramway to Howth and abandon the other alternatives of "horse or other mechanical means of propulsion".

Naturally, this caused much anger in the GNR's camp. The GNR steam trains had served the Howth peninsula unchallenged since 1847, arriving during the famine years and giving much needed employment at a time of great need to the people of Howth. While the GNR were discussing what should be done, the CHHT, in 1896, applied for powers to extend their proposed tramway down from the Summit to link with their proposed Dublin-Howth service at Sutton Cross. The GNR objected in the strongest possible terms to this invasion of their territory, held undisputed for half a century. They argued that, for the CHHT to link Sutton and Howth stations by electric tram was a duplication of their long established service and would lead to loss of revenue. The GNR then put forward their own proposals to run a tram service around the Hill, serving Sutton and Howth and also proposals for the electrification of their branch line from Howth station to Amiens Street (almost a century prior to the arrival of the DART). This latter service would have required single deck electric stock, possibly articulated, to carry peak hour traffic. Whether the GNR were serious or not, the electrification of the railway line was considered by the CHHT to be a direct challenge to their Howth to Nelson's Pillar proposals. The objections of the GNR were upheld and the proposals of the CHHT were rejected. The solution became obvious — both companies withdrew their invasion tactics. The CHHT contented itself with the electric tramway from Clontarf to Howth harbour, which opened in 1900,

The photograph on the top of page 6 was taken midway down the first section of the Harbour East Pier, facing towards the tram terminus with the white terrace in the background. This view is taken from Towerhill, showing the rear pitch of the terrace roofs and one of the Preston cars with trolley turned, ready for the return journey to Dublin.

Courtesy National Tramway Museum, Crich

One of the 1900-built Preston cars, No 304, gleaming in its newness. Note the ornate waist panelling and the curtained windows, conveying a sense of plushness. The bogies are Peckham with the pony wheels leading. The destination board on the rocker panel indicates that the tram is facing towards Dublin. The upper deck surround decency screen advertised the 'Tivoly Theatre'. The livery was ultramarine blue and ivory white.

whilst the GNR built the tramway around the Hill of Howth but dropped plans to electrify their railway.

This book describes both tram systems to serve Howth. In its time the CHHT trams (which ceased operation on 29 March 1941, two years before I was born) were known as the 'Howth Trams', whilst the cars operated by the GNR around the Hill of Howth were known as the 'Hill Trams'. It is important to keep this distinction in mind, though after 1941 the distinction became less significant.

The Howth trams

The Clontarf and Hill of Howth Tramway commenced services on 26 July 1900 and was operated by a fleet of twelve open-top bogie trams built by the Electric Railway and Tramway Carriage Works at Preston in Lancashire, numbered 301-312 inclusive. They seated 30 on the lower deck and 45 on the upper and ran on Peckham maximum traction bogies with the pony (unpowered) wheels leading. When built, they were the largest trams that had appeared up to then in the Dublin area and were the first bogie cars to operate into Dublin city centre. Their enclosed vestibules were much appreciated by the motormen. Other City trams were open-fronted, apart from No 191, an experimental car built in 1899, which had the first enclosed platform in the world and was known as 'the coffin' on account of its angular dash. The new trams soon became known as the 'Preston cars' and were so successful that the DUT in 1906-7, built nine more cars, almost identical except for balcony tops (Nos 294-300, 316/7).

In an effort to raise funds for tram restoration, I often show films and give talks to the various historical societies and senior citizen welfare groups around the city. It was at one of these occasions, after I had been

talking about the Clontarf to Hill of Howth tramroad, that one of the elderly gentlemen came up to me with an interesting snippet of conversation. His name was Willy Brazier and he began speaking about his memories of trams including the item I now wish to relate.

It was about his own father, who at the time, was at school in the old Church of Ireland school house, beside the Ivy Church (St Columba's) in the Strand area of Dublin, and his father's memories were very clear on this instance. The year was 1900 and some two years previously, in 1898, the DUT trams had opened their service from the tram sheds in Clontarf to Nelson's Pillar. There was great excitement in a young boy's mind and it was his local tram that was the first electric tram to reach the Pillar in the great tram building era from 1896, when electrification of the horse tramways had commenced.

For morning break, the boys would gather along the school boundary railings and watch these little cars pass by and all young Brazier wanted at the time, was to be a tram driver. Suddenly, something caught his eye that he was never to forget. Over the hill passing the canal, an apparition appeared, quite different to anything else he had ever witnessed before. He called his friends in loud excitement and soon the railings were thronged with youngsters, hanging on for dear life and the smaller ones pleading to be lifted. The spectacle reduced this small gathering into silence and the end of break bell went unheard. There, just a few feet away, passed twelve of the most magnificent tramcars that they had ever seen, at least twice the size of the little open-fronts that they had been accustomed to. These were, of course, the twelve magnificent, Preston-built vestibuled bogie cars – the first of their sort in the city – passing in slow procession on their way to commence service on the Clontarf to Hill of Howth route. Apparently each tram was carried on a low-loader drawn by several powerful horses, which added to the magic of the occasion. We can get some idea of the scene that morning in 1900 from the picture above, showing the new trams stored at St Anne's reserve. All the boys renewed their determination to become motormen and to power one of these supreme 'kings of the road'.

As mentioned above, the CHHT cars were numbered 301-12 inclusive. This was so that they would not be confused with DUT stock and they were thus able to retain these numbers when taken into DUT stock in 1907. The CHHT originally was operated by its own crews with different uniforms and insignia and a change of crew took place at the commencement of the St Anne's reserve, just beyond Dollymount. This was found tedious and unnecessary and in 1907 it was agreed that the CHHT crews would be absorbed into the DUTC payroll and, hence forward no change of crews took place. The CHHT, however, retained its legal independence throughout its lifetime, although outwardly indistinguishable from the DUTC. It was well within William Martin Murphy's power to buy out the CHHT as he did the DSDT, but for some reason he allowed the CHHT to retain its own identity even though, to an observer, the CHHT appeared to be part of the DUT in terms of staff, uniform, livery, garter etc. In 1905, when the DUT attempted to legally absorb the DSDT, the CHHT objected in an effort to protect their own independence. However, later, negotiations were started and the CHHT offered to lease their line to the DUT for a 99 year period in return for rent. For the year 1907, the DUT would pay £2000; for 1908, £2500; and thereafter £3000 per year. The DUT then became responsible for the supply of tickets, the payment of wages, and the actual running of the service.

In 1907, the DUT provided an internal partition in the saloons of cars 301-312, with one compartment exclusively for smokers and the other for non-smokers. These partitions were removed in 1928. In the period 1918-25, eleven of the cars were rebuilt with new DUT four-windowed saloons and new traction bogies (by Hurst Nelson or Mountain and Gibson) with the pony wheels facing inwards. The only exception was No 308, which was a new tram built in 1920, the original having been destroyed during the Easter

The original No 307 would have appeared exactly as No 304 on page 11. In May 1920, No 307 emerged in its new metamorphosis with four saloon windows and a less rounded windscreen. In May 1931, its Peckham bogies were changed for Hurst Nelson, and it has these latter bogies in this photograph at Clontarf Depot. No 307 is in the green and cream livery introduced in 1935 and bears the No 31 route number. *Southern Counties Touring Society*

Top: No 324, in green and cream livery, at Parkgate Street. This car was built in 1907 as a balcony car but in April 1927 it was converted to a single decker to serve on the Bath Avenue route to Sandymount. In 1932 it was pressed into service on the No 31 route to Howth after being fitted with upper deck seating.

Bottom left: After the closure in 1941, the fleet was kept at Conyingham Road for a while, and later scrapped at Donnybrook depot, where this photograph was taken.

Above: No 310 at the north side of Nelson's Pillar shortly before the closure, with the trolley pole reversed and ready to set off to Howth.

Opposite bottom: This famous tram was nicknamed the ''Submarine', as it was used to negotiate the floods common enough in Dublin at the time. This was because its motors were elevated higher than in other trams. Originally a horse tram, converted to electric in 1900, she was withdrawn in 1938.

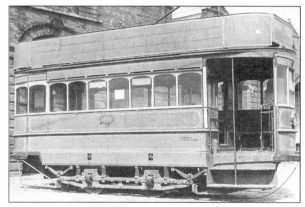

Rising (see page 19-20). Balcony-top and fully-enclosed trams could not operate on the Howth route due to the low overbridges at Clontarf and Howth. When more cars were required in 1932 to supplement the fleet, the DUT converted cars 320, 321 and 324 to open-top. These cars had already been converted from balcony to single deck to negotiate a low bridge on the Bath Avenue to Sandymount line, and all that was necessary was the simple addition of seats and a surround caging.

However, the introduction of the new streamlined 'luxury' bogie cars on the Dalkey route in 1931 provided, for the first time, a fully enclosed car with a low enough roof profile to negotiate these bridges. One was run experimentally to Howth to ensure that it cleared the over bridges. It did, and Nos 280 and 293 were transferred from the Dalkey route. A further five with 'adjusted roofs' were introduced as follows: No 300 (7 March 1933), No 294 (1 April 1933), No 329 (31 March 1934), No 330 (16 April 1934) and No 93 (18 June 1934). One of these, No 294, operated the last tram from Howth on 29 March 1941.

Although the Howth trams ceased operations some two years before I was born, I have distinct memories of their permanent way and route, as no serious disturbance took place until the 1950s, especially along the reserved track at the back of St Anne's Estate. Even today, the undulations of the old sea wall to accomodate passing loops are testimony to this once fine system. In the late 1990s, site works opposite Teeling's motor garage near Howth exposed double track set in cobble stone on the right hand side of the road (going towards Howth) just before the place where the tramway crossed to the left to serve Howth station, and pass by the harbour on its final lap to the terminus at the base of the East Pier.

The Howth trams and the GNR never strayed far from each other. The trams passed by the GNR station at Amiens Street, under the skew bridge at Clontarf which carried the GNR main line over the Clontarf Road, on the level over the Hill tram route at Sutton Cross, and finally under the steel viaduct which carried the Hill trams up over the main road at Howth station. The well known photograph reproduced above was taken in the early days of both systems, outside Howth station facing towards Dublin. The CHHT car is at road level heading towards the city, whereas the GNR car is leaving Howth station towards the Summit. It is obviously a 'staged' photograph, as both tramcars are stationary for the photographer, though some prints of this well known photograph have obliterated the passengers and crews to give the impression that it is an action shot.

At Sutton Cross the two routes crossed on the level and special arrangements had to be made. The CHHT overhead wires stopped just nine inches short of either side of the GNR wire and it was necessary to coast through the break in power. I can recall that the 'Hill trams' always set off a shower of sparks at this crossing and this fascinated me as a child. The rules for priority at the junction were well established. A CHHT car heading towards Dublin had priority over a GNR car at all times, and a GNR car setting off towards Howth Summit had priority over a Howth bound CHHT tram. Originally,

Luxury car No 330 with specially adapted low profile domed roof for the Howth route, standing at the Howth East pier terminus. The building to the right is now the world famous King Sitric restaurant.

there was a compulsory stop enforced on all 'Hill trams' approaching the Cross, but in later years this only applied to Sutton-bound cars. Mishaps at this location were rare indeed.

In spite of their initial misgivings towards each other, the CHHT and GNR had a great deal in common in the early years. They were both operated by massive open-top bogie cars, the first of their kind in the city. Their route mileage differed by only a ¼ mile (excluding the Dollymount to city centre section). They served the same territory, both had mention of the Hill of Howth in their names, and both had maximum traction bogies, with the pony wheels leading in the case of the earlier CHHT cars and numbers 9 and 10 of the GNR Hill of Howth fleet. The two fleets were similar in size (twelve and ten cars respectively) and general appearance, and both were English built.

The two systems also had striking differences which set them well apart. The CHHT travelled entirely on the level, apart from road undulation, when passing through the North Strand and over the Royal Canal. These level areas led to a good turn of speed on long straight sections, especially on the St Anne's Estate lands, now James Larkin Road. The Hill of Howth Tramway on the other hand operated entirely on a hill, apart from the sea level section at the Sutton end. Straight sections were comparatively rare, and never of long duration. The motorman was constantly rising and dropping the notches, and ever vigilant for the many sharp bends and corners. These were so extreme in parts, that double check rails were necessary to prevent derailments.

They also had very different clientele. The Howth trams were heavily used by shoppers and by businessmen heading off to the city for a day's work. The Hill trams, although also used by commuters, were patronised mostly by day trippers, especially during the summer months. The Howth tram operator was a 'driver' whereas the Hill trams were in the control of a 'motorman'. The Howth trams, in the early days, had a divided saloon for smokers, whereas smokers were only permitted on the upper deck of the Hill cars and, even then, behind the trolley. The Howth cars were covered stem to stern with advertisements, frantically selling the necessities of life, whereas the Hill trams seldom carried advertisements, unless for a local jumble sale or a parish fête. The Hill cars usually carried the postman, and waited while he emptied post boxes en route, whereas letters were only carried on an experimental basis for a short period in the 1930s on the Howth cars.

When buses made their presence felt in the 1930s, both the GNR and the DUT chose to provide bus services to outlying areas not served by trams. The GNR introduced a bus service to Malahide (42 A) and the DUT were angered as they previously had intentions to run such a service. The GNR agreed to abandon this service, subject to the DUT abandoning the tram service to Howth, as the GNR had a special interest in this route. An agreement was reached between the parties. However, the DUT had to negotiate with the CHHT, with whom they had a 99 year lease. The service was running at a loss and they were anxious to withdraw from their legal responsibilities. Tram services 23, 24 and 25 had now ceased, and what was the point in paying a lease of £3000 a year for the privilege of running at a loss? The CHHT demanded a bulk payment, equivalent to 14 years rent, and the DUT agreed not only to pay this £42,000, but allow the CHHT to retain the scrap value of the permanent way and overhead cable, etc. This amounted to £3700 extra. The original open-toppers were withdrawn from service around this time and delivered to Donnybrook where they remained in the open until 1941, when they were scrapped.

The last Howth tram left the East Pier terminus at 11.45 pm on 29 March 1941, with motorman Dick Ward at the controls, and were seen off by large crowds of well-wishers. Thus ended a fascinating tramway with its own special character and history, never relinquishing its bid for a separate identity, and having provided a sterling and reliable service for over 40 years.

Going to school by tram

An older professional colleague of mine, Kieran Murphy, has fond memories of the Howth trams and recalls the many pranks he and his school friends would get up to, on their way to and from school. On Saturdays a group of them would set off on an open-top tram to Fairview Park where they would meet friends for a game of football. As with all youngsters, money for sweets was always a problem and they were always seeking ways of finding a few pennies for that extra ice cream or bottle of pop. Whoever had the couple of pence was always assured of 'lasting' friendship. When travelling to school with their heavy schoolbags, Kieran told me that the lads would leave their bags under the slatted seats. Sometimes the problem was remembering them and it was not uncommon for some tearful youngster to stand on the tracks, watching the vacated car trundle

No 303, in blue and white livery, stands at the terminus at Dollymount, with St Anne's Estate to the left and the sea to the right. A neatly dressed school boy sets off for home after leaving the tram. The trees are in full bloom and the scene must be around May or early June.

off into the distance. In school, "Please Sir, I couldn't do my homework as I had left my bag on the tram", was no excuse at all. What Kieran discovered was that there was ample space under the corner seat for a youngster or two to crawl into, depending on their agility and size. One morning, on their way to Fairview Park, Kieran announced that he knew a way to save money for sweets, and they listened eagerly as he explained his proposals. To prove his point he was bundled under the seat with another small friend and his mates sat above them with their togs and bags on their knees and at their feet, to hide them. As the tram groaned and shuddered along, poor Kieran and his friend were rolled from side to side as if in a wrecked ship, and it wasn't long before both of them felt quite seasick. Still, they kept to the plan, the conductor came and collected the fares and as the tram pulled in alongside the park, it was a very relieved group of youngsters that flew, "like bats from hell", off the car to ensure that the conductor had no time for a head count. They celebrated the success of their venture with extra goodies and Kieran and his friend were the heroes of the day. This was repeated a few times until the conductor caught on and that ended up with the sharp edge of his tongue and a clip on the back of the neck. Still it was worth it all!

Jerry O'Brien was born in 1907, attended O'Connell's Christian Brothers' School and travelled to and from school by the tram. He told me several stories associated with the trams and the tricks the youngsters would get up to. But one memory remained steadfastly in his mind over his long years.

He was returning back to Howth from school sitting at the front of one of the splendid open-top Preston cars. As the tram rounded Claremount gates, an amazing sight caught his eyes, dark palls of black smoke curled up into the sky and a ferocious wailing filled the air. Crowds of men and shawled women were scattered on the tracks ahead, re-echoing memories of the Rebellion and the Civil War, of a few short years before. The tram car reduced pace to a crawl as it cautiously proceeded through the throngs of ranting mourners. From the vantage point on the top of the tram, Jerry observed the whole colourful proceedings. There, raised high on an earthen bank beside the tramway, where the Teckrete factory now stands, was the body of a 'travelling man', dressed in fine regalia. And it was for him that the women wailed so woefully. He learnt afterwards that the occasion was the death of their 'king', and all his worldly goods were burnt beside him to enable them to follow him into the next life. It wasn't the death of the king that remained uppermost in Jerry's mind but the poor dead donkey beside him, slaughtered to provide transport for the king in the new world. The whole bizarre scenario struck Jerry as a little biblical, but what haunted his memory most were two sayings that existed at the time "as rare as a dead tinker king", and "as rare as a dead donkey". Here both sayings merged as one.

Footprints in the sand

It was common for people to leave packages on the trams for delivery to the city where they were picked up. Children often travelled unescorted, to be picked up by an aunt or uncle for a day's outing to the zoo. At one time, there was no cobbler in Howth and parents would ask the conductor to transport shoe boxes of damp sand and hand them in to a particular shoe maker near the Pillar. The damp sand accurately carried the imprint of the child's foot and it is said that a good cobbler could tell from the impression whether a special shoe was required to correct some imperfection in the child's foot. I have also heard this story associated with the famous Blessington steam tramway and so perhaps, all long distance routes have similar experiences of one sort or another.

Bert (Harold) Brown, the oldest member of the tram restoration team, who is now 80 years of age, (1998) remembers the 'post office tram'. A post box was fitted on both platforms of a Howth tram and passengers could drop in a card or letter when in transit or as the tram stopped at Howth. The contents were emptied by a member of the company who simply crossed O'Connell Street to deliver them to the GPO, which was situated almost opposite the Pillar. I am told that it was not uncommon for a passenger to fill in, stamp and post a card while in transit.

Bert also remembers cycling home to Sutton and passing the Clontarf tram depot and noticing a strange looking open-top tram. It was an unusual bottle green colour, was numberless and had a highly ornate upper deck surround caging. On entering the tram he realised that this was no ordinary vehicle. It was adorned with plush cushioned swivel seating, carved cherubs, intricate woodwork lacing and a drinks cabinet in the saloon. The upper deck was also richly appointed and he noticed the absence of a decency screen so commonplace on all other open-top trams. It was of course the 'directors' tram' and as all directors were 'gentlemen', what need of decency boarding? The extravagance of detail left a lasting impression on Bert's mind.

Concerning the Howth to Dublin tram, I would also like to tell a short story, to the best of my knowledge, previously untold. It was related to me by the late John Byrne, who lived in Cheancor Road at the time. When he was a lad, some time during the First World War, he was on his way to school by tram and boarded the city bound car at Sutton Cross having travelled down hill from Cheancor Road by one of the 'Hill cars'. After a while he heard a strange wailing on the open upper deck like no sound he had ever heard before. It was high pitched, hollow and eerie. He could hold his curiosity no longer and ran upstairs to see what was the cause of these strange sounds. He found a small child, about four or five years old, with his anxious parents trying to console him. When John moved closer to learn the cause of the problem, he discovered that the child

A side view of the numberless Directors' tram (1901) in its bottle green and white livery. Notice the provision of only a foot plate, in lieu of the usual decency screen or boarding. The Pont Lorain/Brierly truck was unique. *H Fayle, courtesy IRRS*

had been playing 'soldiers' with a ceramic chamber pot on his head. This had slipped down over his skull and could not be retrieved. The poor lad was frantic in his darkened trap and could not be pacified, and was on his way to the Mater Hospital to have it 'surgically' removed. The conductor who had been collecting fares in the saloon now mounted the stairs and quickly retreated, returning with a large brass switch key. He studied the 'po' for some moments and then applied a quick tap of the key and the 'po' came away in two clean halves. He announced that the very same thing had happened to his own son some weeks previously and he had seen the method of release. It is difficult to imagine what would have happened had the 'po' fractured into many sharp pieces, injuring the child. The company would have been liable and the conductor could have lost his job. He took a chance and fortunately it paid off. The much relieved family continued their journey to the city and decided to visit the zoo to help the youngster forget his trauma.

The Howth gun-running

There was a famous incident in the troubled history of Ireland, shortly before our independence from England, known as the 'Howth Gun Running'. This took place on the last Sunday of July 1914. A yacht called the *Asgard* sailed into Howth harbour, captained by her owner Erskine Childers and loaded with a cargo of guns for the Nationalist Volunteers. In defiant mood, the Volunteers, in the early hours of the morning, marched boldly into Dublin bearing arms. The authorities, on hearing that a gun-running boat had arrived in Howth,

No 308, circa 1913, outside Clontarf Depot with the crew standing by.

immediately commandeered the Clontarf trams and set off at a brisk speed for Howth, to intercept the rebels. It seems that the forces on the trams arrived too late, as the Volunteers had long gone. They immediately beat a hasty retreat back to Dublin, but, the great 'tram chase' arrived too late; the Volunteers had long since dispersed with their weapons. There was great jubilation in the camp of the Volunteers that night and a lot of red faces among the authorities of the day.

One tram that might well have taken part in the chase was car No 308, built at Preston. During the Rising of 1916, the British forces brought *HMS Helga*, a gunboat, up the Liffey and trained it on the main thoroughfare of O'Connell Street. *Helga* bombarded the city for many hours and poor No 308, it is said, took a direct hit in North Earl Street and lay in a crumpled heap. It would seem that the crown forces had in some manner redeemed the ignominious tram chase of two years previously. But, not to be outdone, the insurgents hastily erected barricades around the stricken tram and so No 308, in her dying throes, served the Nationalist cause once again.

Top right: The loop at Kilbarrick is still in evidence today. This view is looking towards the city.

Bob Dawson

Top left: The remains of tram No 308 after the Easter Rising. It was replaced by a new open-top car of the same number in 1920.

Above: The route of the CHHT is still evident outside the Transport Museum. The tram kept to the right along the stone wall past the castle gate and church, before crossing the road to serve Howth station. *James Kilroy*

Right: Luxury tram No 294 was the last car to operate the Howth to Dublin service on 29 March 1941.

The Hill of Howth Tramway

As described earlier, the GNR tramway round the Hill of Howth was built in response to the perceived 'invading' tactics of the Clontarf and Hill of Howth Tramway. The GNR Hill of Howth Electric Tramway was opened on 17 June 1901 and, like the Howth trams, ran on the Irish standard gauge of five foot three inches. The first batch of eight trams (Nos 1-8) was delivered in 1901 and was built by Brush Electric. They had Brill 22-E bogies, carried 67 passengers and were turned out in a livery of crimson lake and ivory, gaily lined out with gold. Originally the open decks had low caging around them but, on account of the many lineside trees and the proximity of the traction poles, it was decided to double the height of the caging, making these the highest open-topped trams in the world.

A convoy of three cars at Sutton station, ready to set out for Howth Summit. The trams are in the original crimson and cream (blood and custard) livery and the vestibules are open. The first car is full, the second is 'loading' while the third car awaits passengers. The window blinds are partially dropped, but the strangest thing of all is that each car carries an advertisement on the platform step. This was a very rare occurrence. The notice on the front dash reads 'Car to follow', in blue letters on a white background.

Courtesy National Tramway Museum, Crich

The following year the company purchased two further cars (Nos 9-10) designed at their workshops in Dundalk and built by G F Milnes on Peckham 14D-5 bogies with a carrying capacity of 73 passengers. These were built specifically for summer traffic and had some features reflecting railway carriage design. They had open windows originally, and looked quite different from the first batch, if not less modern in appearance. On account of their larger railway proportions, they were much higher and heavier than the earlier cars and were quite unsuited to the steep turns and gradients on the Summit to Howth section. They were used only at times of peak traffic and then only on the Sutton to the Summit section, avoiding the steep section between the Summit and Howth.

The sharp curves also caused problems with the first batch and derailments were frequent in the early years until massive diagonally fixed springs, linking the bogies, prevented the outward thrust which caused derailment. These were known as 'cross springs' and no other tram system had such springs. When cars Nos 5 and 8 were withdrawn from service in 1958, their cross springs were fitted to Nos 9 and 10 from the second batch, and for their last season these fine cars could then safely descend the hill from the Summit into Howth railway station, the steepest section of the line. As a precaution, they were managed by only the most experienced motormen.

By the First World War, the cars were sorely in need of repainting. However, on account of the shortage

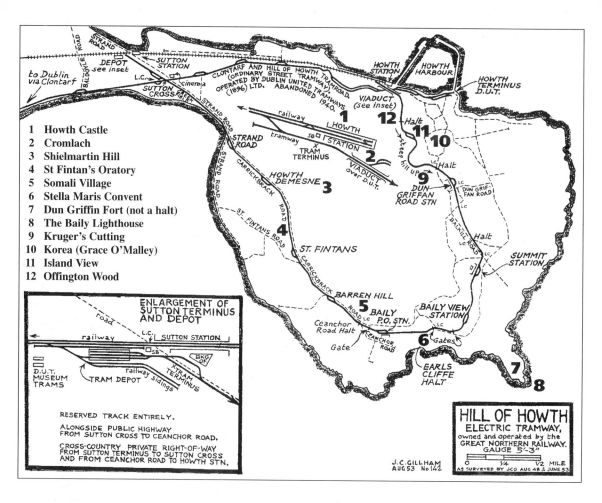

1 Howth Castle
2 Cromlach
3 Shielmartin Hill
4 St Fintan's Oratory
5 Somali Village
6 Stella Maris Convent
7 Dun Griffin Fort (not a halt)
8 The Baily Lighthouse
9 Kruger's Cutting
10 Korea (Grace O'Malley)
11 Island View
12 Offington Wood

ENLARGEMENT OF SUTTON TERMINUS AND DEPOT

D.U.T. MUSEUM TRAMS
TRAM DEPOT
railway sidings
X TRAM TERMINUS
L.C. SUTTON STATION
railway
road
SB
BKG. OF.

RESERVED TRACK ENTIRELY.

ALONGSIDE PUBLIC HIGHWAY FROM SUTTON CROSS TO CEANCHOR ROAD.

CROSS-COUNTRY PRIVATE RIGHT-OF-WAY FROM SUTTON TERMINUS TO SUTTON CROSS AND FROM CEANCHOR ROAD TO HOWTH STN.

J.C.GILLHAM AUG 53 No 142

HILL OF HOWTH ELECTRIC TRAMWAY,
owned and operated by the GREAT NORTHERN RAILWAY.
GAUGE 5'-3"
0   1/4   1/2 MILE
AS SURVEYED BY JCG AUG 48 & JUNE 53

Two of the Brush cars, Nos 1 and 3, in crimson and cream livery, standing at Howth station, with the Station Master's house seen to the right of No 1. It will be necessary to reverse the trolley of No 1 for the return journey to Sutton. No 1 is bedecked with Japanese, French and other flags, celebrating the armistice in 1918. Japan was on the side of the 'allies' in the First World War. Notice the smart appearance of the French style uniform of the two crew standing at the dash.

Courtesy National Tramway Museum, Crich

No 4 at the Summit around 1904. The waiting room with seat is to the right. 'The Pavilion' is located on higher ground to the left, where tea or light refreshments were served to the passengers to the accompaniment of a band in high season. The Pavilion was burnt down in August 1918 and brick houses now cover the spot.

W Lawrence, courtesy National Tramway Museum, Crich

of pigments resulting from the war, the company adopted the grained mahogany varnished livery, used on its carriages, for all its tramcars. Varnish is not as effective as oil-based paint for protecting woodwork and, correctly speaking, a light sanding and revarnish at frequent intervals was necessary. Unless this is done, especially when in daily use, the varnish would flake and the wood discolour. In the 1930s, when repainting was again necessary, the company chose a livery of Oxford blue and cream, already used on its buses and railcars. It should be kept in mind that the specification for the mahogany livery involved eighteen applications in all. As Nos 9 and 10 were so seldom used, they did not need a full repaint and retained the grained mahogany appearance to the end.

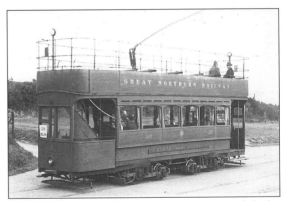

No 5, at the exact same location some years later, is in the grained mahogany livery introduced during the First World War.

Courtesy National Tramway Museum, Crich

Route description

The tram depot was located at Baldoyle on lands just west of Sutton and Baldoyle railway station. The depot was a large timber structure with three lines of tracks opening to a fan in the yard in front. Originally the three massive shed doors were hinged and outward opening but, in high winds, were known to slam closed and damage emerging trams, so they were replaced with sliding doors after a number of years. An adjoining brick

No 8, in crimson and cream livery, ascending from Howth Station with Ireland's eye split in two by the trolley. The traction poles are on the seaward side. This general area was known as 'Island View'.

Courtesy National Tramway Museum, Crich

building contained the powerhouse with tall chimney which remained a landmark for many years after the closure and the powerhouse is now the home for the Akzo Nobel paint factory, originally known as Parsons. A smaller battery house was constructed at the Summit to act as a boosting station during periods of heavy demand, and night running was fed from this source. The line was a typical single track layout with passing loops at approximately half mile intervals where ascending cars passed descending cars, the former always keeping to the left. The trams travelled on their own reserve of bullhead rail with sleepers, and grooved tramway rail in cobblestones was only used where public roads were crossed. At times the reserve track followed the existing road, keeping to the seaward side except for a small section at Stella Maris convent. When the serious climbs began, the trams departed from the roads to make their own way through heretofore untouched terrain. The section from the Summit to Howth railway station was entirely on tramroad reserve, parting company from the early network of small roads and lanes.

Sutton

On leaving the depot, or shed, at Baldoyle the tram crossed Station Road to enter Sutton and Baldoyle station yard and pick up passengers from the trains. Leaving the station, the trams crossed back over Station Road and travelled along the right hand side margin, on their own walled-in reserve, as far as Sutton Cross. This reserve is now a linear strip of grass, its origins no longer obvious. Sutton crossroads was an interesting place where trams were concerned. It was where the Hill trams crossed over the route of the Howth to Dublin cars, until the closure of the latter system in 1941. Up until then the latter cars were named the 'Howth trams', following the tradition of using the outer terminus to name the route. After 1941, the 'Hill trams' gradually became known as the 'Howth trams', as there were no longer any need to make a distinction.

Sutton to the Summit

Beyond the Cross, the trams set off keeping to the right hand side past the Marine Hotel (previously known as the Strand Hotel and earlier still the Golfers' Hotel), until the sea was reached at Strand Road. Ten thousand years previously Howth was an island and at this point the trams were crossing over a section that was originally sea bed. The remains of early stone implements, kitchen middens and mounds of empty shells, once found abundantly along this stretch, were a constant reminder of the early settlers. By Church Lane, originally known as Sax Lane, the tram would once more arrive back on terra firma and the hill climb would begin in earnest. Here the ruined Norman tower, known as Corr Castle, could be seen to the left.

The overall route was a slow, anticlockwise curve rising for the first half in a horseshoe pattern until the Summit and then a gradual downward curve to Howth Station, passing over the main road by a steel bridge or viaduct, the stone supports of which can still be seen. The sea was always to the right, when travelling from Sutton, as were most of the tram poles, and the main hills were always to the left. There has long been a tendency for Howth folk to exaggerate and some rather obscure hills and heathlands are called the 'East

Top: No 1 is about to cross Station Road and enter Sutton and Baldoyle railway station forecourt to pick up passengers. The return track from the reserve on the right hand side of Station Road can be seen in the foreground as it joins the outward bound track. At this crossing it was necessary to edge forward carefully sounding the foot gong.

R J S Wiseman

Centre: A steam train standing at Sutton and Baldoyle railway station, with the locomotive in reverse. In the railway forecourt, one of the blue and cream cars is ready to set off for the Summit. From 1912, the GNR always referred to the Summit halt as the 'Hill of Howth'. The roof over the bridge was later removed, as can be seen in the background of the photo on page 35.

Courtesy National Tramway Museum, Crich

Bottom: Towards the closure, No 1 can be seen passing Sutton Cross on the return journey to Sutton. The 'modern' bus stop erected by CIE can be seen to the right outside the Marine Hotel. Sutton Cinema in the background is now the Headquarters of Superquinn.

Courtesy National Tramway Museum, Crich

An early study taken at Barren Hill under the impressive Shielmartin Hill. Some of the crew on the upper deck are standing on the seats, posing for their photograph. Four tents can be seen half way up the hill. The trees in full foliage, and the long meadow grass, suggest mid summer.

Brian Boyle collection

Mountain', the 'Middle Mountain', and the 'West Mountain'. None of these were mountains in the true sense and Shielmartin hill (560 feet), with its prehistoric cairn, is the only real and distinctive hill.

The climb from Church Lane to the Hill of Howth Summit was gradual with some small valleys in between. St Fintan's graveyard and ruined church (on a site dating from the seventh century) are close to the track, and are located at the base of Shielmartin Hill. The 'Middle Mountain' and Redrock bathing place are beyond the graveyard. The trams travelled along the roadside until Ceanchor Road (which leads to the townland of Censure) was reached. This was the area known as the Baily and was approximately two-thirds of the way between Sutton Cross and the Summit. The tram now entered its own reserved track as far as the Summit and, apart from a small section at Stella Maris convent, avoided the public roadway. It is along these elevated and winding stretches that some of the finest maritime scenery in the Dublin area can be seen and many of the views in all directions are breathtaking. Perched on the upper deck of a swaying old tram, sailing along at rooftop level on your magic wooden carpet, was an experience never to be forgotten. The cheerful holiday crowds were often stunned into silence by the rugged and natural beauty along this steady climb. From the Baily Green could be seen the ancient lighthouse built in 1667 by royal assent of Charles II and located in the fog belt so that it could never be seen when needed. This is now a domestic dwelling called the Beacon, but was originally known as Baily cottage. From here looking down towards the sea, the replacement lighthouse, built in 1818, still survives, although now fully automated. It sits astride the Dun (or Fort) of King Griffin (Criomthain or Crimthan), a famous King who ruled from his Howth eyrie around the time of Christ. He was the last Milesian King of Leinster and later High King of all Ireland and is said to have died in 9 AD. The Milesians were an early Celtic tribe called Clann na Mil (family of Mil) who were believed to have arrived in Ireland at the time of Moses (c1300 BC). Mil was revered as a powerful god.

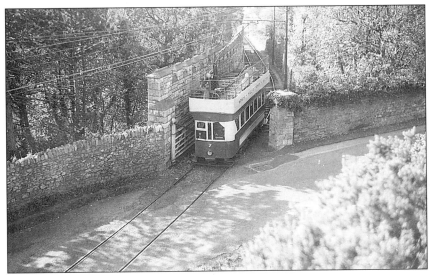

Car No 7 emerging from Stella Maris reserve underneath the battlement walls, built to preserve the privacy of the Convent from inquisitive passengers from the upper deck of the tram. The gate supports and holding tie-hook are still in position. The photograph is taken from the Hill on the opposite side of the road on 14 October 1956 and the tram will now cross over to the left hand side.
J H Price, Courtesy National Tramway Museum, Crich

The Summit to Howth

The main stop en route was the Summit (known officially as 'Hill of Howth') where the holiday crowds would leave the tram and set off on the many walks into the hills and towards the cliffs. With a new complement of passengers, the tram now commenced its final descent, past Howth village on the right hand side, to Howth railway station. The passengers then alighted to join the steam trains or rail-cars for their final return back to Dublin city. In all, they had witnessed some of the most spectacular scenery along the east coast of Ireland, steeped in a richness of memory and history — truly a journey into the past. At Howth passengers could marvel at the seaward

This scene is from a popular (touched-up) postcard which appeared in the mid 1930s showing No 1 in its grained mahogany livery. The tram is exiting from the Summit reserve and has just passed the gate keepers cottage. The track is on the left hand side of Carrick-brack Road and will shortly cross over to pass by the battlemented wall shown in the upper photograph. *Courtesy National Tramway Museum, Crich*

views over north County Dublin, the islands of Ireland's Eye and Lambay and, on a clear day, the famous Mountains of Mourne could be observed in the distance. Approaching the station, there were glimpses of the Norman castle which replaced an earlier timber fortress. This fortress was built in 1177 by a brave Norman knight, Almeric Tristram, who with his comrades fought a contingent of the Danish and Irish residents to conquer Howth on the feast day of St Lawrence. He adopted the good saint's name as a measure of his gratitude. The (Gaisford) St Lawrence family live in the castle to this very day. On Ireland's Eye could be seen one of the many round Martello Towers, built in 1807 along the east coast of Ireland to ward off a Napoleonic attack, which never came. Not far from the tower is the ruined oratory of St Nessan. One of the Earls of Howth wanted to see this sixth century ruin more clearly from his castle window, so he had it shifted stone by stone, making it effectively an archeological forgery.

The winter of 1946/7

Tom Redmond, known as 'The Colonel', told me this story about the tramway. Tom was motorman on the old GNR and has many fond memories. During the winter of 1946/47 the weather conditions were very poor, the worst in Tom's living memory. It had snowed almost non-stop for many weeks and it was reported that even freight trains had been abandoned and totally covered with snow with days often needed to dig them out. (I can recall this winter and my mother asking me to fill the kettle for a pot of tea. I quickly learnt that scooping the snow up in the kettle was inadequate for, though the kettle appeared full, the snow melted and considerably reduced in size! It took many scoops and a long period of waiting for the melt down.) Tom learnt a simple trick to keep the trams running. After a heavy snowfall, the permanent way men, porters, and all the available hands, were called out at night time to shovel up the snow and to discard it in ever growing heaps along the side of the track. There was no difficulty in providing the tram service the next morning, as the tracks were freshly cleared. However, day time falls were a different matter. Worst of all were the late evening falls, as these tended to freeze up the tracks and the uphill climb from Howth often became an impossibility. Tom knew this only too well. Descending from the Summit to Howth in the snowfall could mean an abandoned tram.

It was Tom's wife who provided the solution. Each evening at home, she brushed away the fresh snow, especially last thing at night. This would mean that the overnight freeze would not result in ice and a slippery path. Tom knew that the same principle could apply to the trams and he asked Christie Hanway (known as 'The Manager'), to fit 'brushes' to the trams. Christie was the maintenance man and could turn his hand to anything, As an electrician, he had been fitting 'brushes' to the tram motors for many years and could not at first apprehend Tom's request, "I mean *sweeping* brushes", clarified Tom. Next morning, No 1 left the depot fitted with two sweeping brushes, bolted with brackets to the tram trucks. After a few attempts and modifications, brushes which could be pushed forward, or retracted, were successfully tried and, when advancing, removed fresh snowfalls off the track. A slight tilt outwards at the head of the brush proved very successful and there were no more problems with slippage on ice. Not all the trams were fitted with brushes – only those that would be in service in evening snow conditions. The trials were a great success and Tom was applauded for his innovative proposals. He refused the plaudits directly and passed the credit on to his wife. When the domestic brushes were decommissioned, they were

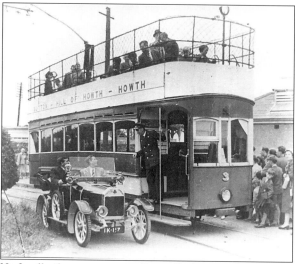

No 3 collecting passengers at Sutton Station near the closure. The motorman, Tommy Wheelan ('rubber neck') is having a chat with passengers in another vehicle of respectable vintage.

At Sutton station on the last day of running, 31 May 1959. If Dubliners had supported the trams so enthusiastically throughout the years, the need for closure would not have arisen.

The Summit Inn today   *James Kilroy*

One of the blue and cream cars setting off to the Summit in August 1952. The tracks of the Dublin to Howth trams are still intact, as they cross from the right hand side to serve Howth Station just beyond the steel bridge.   *R J S Wiseman*

Stella Maris viaduct today. This impressive buttressed stone viaduct brought the tram over 'Glenaveena' valley with an underpass leading to the convent's kitchen garden.   *James Kilroy*

presented to Mrs Redmond with the compliments of the company. This gives a whole new meaning to the name 'Brush Electric', the builders of the tram cars in question!

A number of years ago I brought out a book *Howth and her Trams* which was a collection of short stories and anecdotes associated with the Hill of Howth trams. Some years previous to this, Clifton Flewitt, well known in tramway and railway circles, published an historical and technical book on the system, called *The Hill of Howth Tramway*, with plenty of photographs and drawings. When my own book came out, to avoid repetition, I kept the book light-hearted and without photographs. I was criticised by several people for my flippant approach in dealing with such a fondly remembered and much loved tramway and the absence of photographic material was keenly felt. I am hopeful that this new book will now redeem me in the eyes of my critics.

A short circuit

Several stories were left untold in *Howth and her Trams* due to space and I would like to recount one here. It is a little rude but absolutely true. Motorman Billy McNally, or 'Billy Mac' to all his friends, told me the story about one of his conductors, who I shall decline to name on account of the embarrassing nature of the incident. One late drizzly evening, Billy Mac was descending from the bridge into Howth station. It would have been customary for him to halt his tram outside the little shop called 'The Enterprise', where

This photograph clearly shows the true function of the tramway in serving the station at Howth and picking up passengers. Those wishing to travel on the tram would pass through a gate in the dividing wall. The track setting off can be seen to climb rapidly and the steel viaduct can just be seen ahead. This 1959 view shows one of the new BUT diesel trains introduced by the GNR in 1957-8.

James Kilroy collection

there was good public lighting. It was also customary for the crew to stop off at Gaffney's 'Summit Inn' for a pint, to relieve the dreary winter run, and on this account his conductor whispered to Billy to "drive the tram further down the track into the shadows" as he needed to take a leak. There were no passengers and the station yard was soul-less, so Billy responded to his buddy's request. What he was not to know was that the little used section of track beyond 'The Enterprise' had become overgrown and clogged with mud and the tram was marginally raised above the tracks losing contact with the rails.

A knowledge of electricity would help the understanding of this incident and it is important to realise that electricity must run in an unbroken circuit. The overhead cable provides the outward current which descends the trolley pole to power the motors and then travels through the trucks and wheels to make contact with the rails. The rails are bonded together with copper strips and they provide the return route for the current going back to the power house. Losing contact with the rails, the tram body was 'live' and the poor conductor was unaware of this. Now, we all learnt at school that water is an excellent conductor and when contact was made with the wheels, the home bound current took a short cut . . . to the unfortunate tram conductor! Billy Mac heard his friend's groans of pain and found him curled up, rolling in agony beside the tram. It is said that the poor man did not walk straight again for many days. No doubt the fellow never forgot his unexpected lesson in basic electricity. It took a following tram to haul Billy Mac's tram back on track.

The closure

At the time of their closure, on the 31 May 1959, the Hill of Howth trams were not only the highest, but also the last fleet of open-top trams operating in the world. On the last day of running, No 1 was in the controls of 'Colonel' Tom Redmond, with Willy O'Brien as conductor. No 1 had the honour of being the last tram to leave Howth station on that fateful night and complete the circuit back to Sutton. Throughout the day No1 had been running between the Summit and Howth station, either running with gravity downhill, or labouring under a full load uphill all the way back to the Summit. Tom knew that this would overheat the motors and soon the resistors were smoking gently. Tom complained to the supervisor who was a CIE official who knew nothing about trams and was only knowledgeable about buses. Tom explained that a long run down to Sutton was necessary to cool down the resistors, but the official refused. After all, trams were shortly to be a thing of the past and what was the point of breaking time schedules for reasons of sentiment. It nearly broke Tom's heart to feel his faithful charge burning up and struggling for survival. Finally, No 1 was permitted down to Sutton and the motors which were quietly sizzling by this time finally cooled down, albeit for the last time.

Preservation

Sadly the trams are no more, but their memory still lives on. In all, four of the fleet of ten Hill of Howth trams have survived. Two of these are from the first batch of eight. The tram to make the inaugural run on 17 June 1901, No 4, has survived and can be seen at the Ulster Folk and Transport Museum at Cultra in Northern Ireland. No 2 is running once more, regauged to 4'8½", at the Orange Museum in Perris, California. In addition, the bogies and control gear of No 6 are now under Manchester 'Californian' type single-deck car no 765, operating at Heaton Park Museum, Manchester.

Both of the heavier mahogany painted cars have survived. Tram No 9 (Ireland's last tram) was rescued from the brink of oblivion and is now restored and on display at the National Transport Museum in the grounds of Howth castle, where a collection of fascinating and rare vehicles are on view. It is hoped that one day No 9 will be put into service around Howth Castle estate and perhaps passengers will again enjoy the pleasure of a tram ride around the Hill of Howth. No 10, also regauged to 4'8½", having spent some time running in Blackpool, is now on display at the National Tramway Museum at Crich, Derbyshire. Car No 3, known as the 'Christmas tram', as she was decorated with fairy lights, tinsel and holly each December, and the works car, No 11, were also set aside for preservation, but sadly, vandalism and the elements prevented the realisation of this dream. With four complete trams, and the running parts of a fifth, surviving out of a fleet of ten passenger trams, a survival rate of nearly 50% is unusual in itself. It is not only testimony to their uniqueness, but reflects the great world wide affection and high esteem with which this small but scenic seaside route was held. Sadly none of the CHHT cars survived.

The tram team has changed many times over the years as workers come and go; only Eddie the painter and Brian Greene go back almost to the beginning. Eddie and Brian's standard of paintmanship is second to none and a glimpse at the finish of No 9 from the Hill of Howth, will testify to this. John Kelleher does all the steel work and deals with all the difficult technical problems. John Wheatly must also be mentioned for his hard work in this direction also. Kevin Carlton was known as 'Lord of the Underworld' as it took a man of his unending patience, to scrub clean and paint the underside of No 9. A pair of feet sticking out was the only evidence of his silent work over many months. Bert Brown, our oldest member at 80 years, is our electrician and as someone once said, "If there was no Bert, you would have to invent him". It is amazing at the number of helpers whose Christian names begin with the letter 'B'. Brian, Bert, Brendan, Bill and Bob. Bob is most reliable, rarely missing a Saturday, and he is our official photographer, many of his photographs adorning this book. The quietest member must have been Johnny Grace, now married and living in Portugal. Others come and go, John, Philip, Dermot, Helena and many, many others. I thank all these workers for the years of dedicated effort, without whose help there would be no restored trams. This book is dedicated to them.

Brendan McGuire is the newest acquisition to the 'Tram Restoration Team'. He is seen here sanding the inner side of the upper deck decency screen boarding of open-top car No 224. Sanding is tiring work but cannot be avoided.
Bob Dawson

Brian Greene using wet abrasive on the upperdeck screen of No 224.
Bob Dawson

Bob Dawson preparing the stairs for an undercoat. Bob seldom misses a Saturday.
James Kilroy

Bert (Harold) Brown, seen fitting the lighting into No 224. At 80 years of age Bert is our oldest member.
Bob Dawson

John Kelleher constructed the upper surround caging for Hill of Howth No 9, and is seen here doing the same for No 224.
Bob Dawson

Hill of Howth trams in colour

The Clontarf and Hill of Howth Tramway closed before colour photography became common and indeed colour photographs of any Dublin trams are rare. However, we begin with this typical scene at Nelson's Pillar in 1949, shortly before the closure of Dublin's tram system, with the bus making its presence keenly felt. The balcony car in the foreground saw continuous service from the first decade of the century to closure in 1949. I can recall sitting at the front balcony with a fresh wind all the way to Dalkey, an exhilarating experience. The four wheel 'luxury' car in the background, No 132, was constructed in 1935 with a Maley and Taunton truck and 60 seats. After the closure, she was set aside for preservation by the Transport and Science Museum (the forerunner of the National Transport Museum at Howth). However, due to the uncaring public attitude towards preservation at the time, she could not be saved. She spent her last years adjacent to the GNR tram depot at Sutton, suffering constantly from vandalism and was finally pushed into a quarry behind the Elfin public house, where houses now stand.

W E Robertson, ColourRail

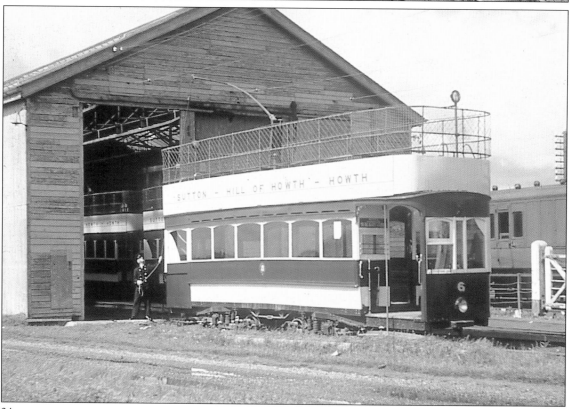

Opposite top: Car No 7 outside Sutton tram depot. On the right of the shed is a carriage siding used by the GNR to store old coaches that were retained for seasonal use. These appear in the background of most photos at Sutton depot and in this view an Edwardian clerestory vehicle is visible. The furnace chimney of the power plant can be seen above the roof of the tram shed. Until its demolition around 1966, it vied with Nelson's Pillar in terms of height and grandeur. It is coincidental that both Howth and Hill of Howth trams terminated under similarly tall structures.

R L Ludgate

Opposite bottom: In this August 1956 scene, No 6 is outside the depot and two other blue and cream cars are visible inside. The railway carriage in the background is an ex-LNWR brake third, purchased in 1947 from the LMS in England and re-guaged for the GNR. The conductor is in the process of reversing the trolley pole for the Howth-bound return journey. Note the lettering along the upper deck of the tram. Trams were orientated so that the end saying 'Howth' was towards Howth at all times and vice versa. In fact the crew spoke about the 'Howth' or 'Sutton' end of a tram.

C B C, ColourRail

Above: Taken on the same day as the picture on the left, this is a lovely view of No 10, gleaming after a recent shower of rain. Again we are outside the Sutton tram sheds but looking in the opposite direction towards the station. The trolley has been turned and No 10 awaits the arrival of her crew, before setting off on her journey around the Hill. Car No 2 is approaching, having completed its tour of duty. The buffer stops of the carriage siding are visible in front of the signal cabin and behind No 2 is the footbridge over Sutton and Baldoyle station. Note that the bridge roof, seen on page 25, is now gone. To the left of the cabin the white gates of the railway level crossing over Station Road are visible. When ready, No 10 will proceed over Station Road to the station yard to pick up its passengers.   *C B C, ColourRail*

Opposite top: Car No 9 has entered Sutton and Baldoyle station yard by crossing Station Road from the tram depot, out of view behind the tram. It has loaded its passengers and is ready to depart. Christy Hanway is poised at the controls and a lady (possibly the photographer's wife) poses for her photograph on the rear platform. Sutton and Baldoyle station building is to the right hand side, just outside the photograph and the Up starting signal on the platform is visible. This May 1959 photograph appeared for the first time on the cover of my earlier book *Irish Trams*, which was published in 1996. Soon after, I received a delightful phone call from a Mrs Noelle Bruton, who had immediately recognised her parents on the front upper deck. Her father, James Masterson, is the gentleman with the red tie. He worked for The Irish Independent Newspapers and Mrs Masterson is by his side. Sometimes the people in the photographs are more important than the actual subject itself. *M J O'Connor, courtesy National Tramway Museum, Crich, Derbyshire*

Opposite bottom: This is the cover shot, reproduced in full. Car No 6 is standing outside Sutton station to pick up its passengers, at the same point as the top view but looking in the opposite direction towards Sutton Cross. The track here forms a clockwise loop and, on exiting the station yard, will recross the road and enter a reserve of track on the right hand side of Station Road, as far as Sutton Cross (see below). The chimney to the right of the tram pole belongs to the Station Master's house, then occupied by Mr O'Neill. Sutton and Baldoyle station building is to the left of the picture. An eager crowd of women are in the process of boarding the tram. The flowers or shrubs in front of the station building are in full bloom which, along with the coats, suggests a spring view. *R L Ludgate*

Above: This shot clearly shows car No 2, leaving the station yard at Sutton to cross back over Station Road on 2 October 1953. The tram will then swing left, onto the section of reserved track, which runs alongside Station Road on the right hand side, as far as Sutton Cross. On the return journey the tram will continue along the reserved track, passing the break in the wall shown here, and, after reversing the trolley, re-enter the station from the opposite end. A car coming out of service would stop on the reserve at a midway point between the entrance and exit breaks in the reserve boundary wall to set down passengers at a conveniently located pedestrian gate, through which they could cross to the station. This avoided a change of the trolley just to re-enter Sutton and Baldoyle station yard. *W E Robertson, ColourRail*

Opposite top: This scene is something of a mystery and shows No 6 on the reserve section beyond the station exit gate and apparently heading towards the Cross. No 4 is simultaneously seen exiting from Sutton and Baldoyle station yard and both trams have passengers. No 6 will need to move forward to permit No 4 onto the reserve track, otherwise No 4 would cause a blockage on Station Road. The scene would make more sense if No 6 were returning from the Summit and travelling in the direction of the tram sheds, but the motorman can be seen in his vestibule and the trolley is set for travelling towards the Cross. It is possible, of course, that Nos 4 and 6 are to travel together in convoy and that No 6 reversed as soon as it crossed Station Road and sat waiting for No 4 to catch up. If this is the case, the leading car would have a display panel saying, 'car to follow' on the dash. It certainly is not a typical view.   *R L Ludgate*

Opposite bottom: No 3 is passing over Sutton Crossroads and is about to pass over the cobble stoned tracks of the Dublin to Howth tram, defunct since 1941. The tram has a pretty full complement of passengers and a car in the distance is returning back to the tram sheds. There is a passing loop to the left, just beyond the traction pole and the pole itself also acts as a telegraph pole. The car setting out, in this case No 3, would have had a straight run through the loop, whereas the returning car ahead would have swerved left onto the passing section of track. Correctly speaking, the passengers on the upper deck should be in a seated position, but perhaps they are standing to search their pockets for the fare.   *R L Ludgate*

Above: On 2 October 1953, car No 3 is in the process of exiting from the loop at Strand Road and is about to rejoin the main track towards Sutton Crossroads. On the right are the lands of Santa Sabina Convent, whose pupils frequently travelled on the trams. On the left, beyond the road junction, was the most exposed section of track. In stormy conditions and with a full tide, the wind would whip up the spray and lash the side of the passing trams. On setting off to the Summit, the motorman would retreat upstairs to avoid being drenched, having notched-up the tram to coast through this exposed section. On the return journey to Sutton, the conductor usually stayed in his saloon to avoid a wetting.

W E Robertson, ColourRail

Opposite top: No 4 has stopped at Barren Hill loop on an upward journey towards the Summit and the section lamp on the pole has now been switched to clear the section ahead, as far as the Baily Post Office. This procedure was to prevent two cars meeting on a single section of track between passing loops. While this could happen, it was quite rare and was caused by opposing section lamps being switched simultaneously and the motorman failing to notice the cancellation of his lamp. Usually, whoever had travelled the furthest had a gentleman's right of way or, sometimes, an empty car would reverse to avoid disruption to the passengers on a full tram. Barren Hill loop projected into the public road causing a bottleneck in heavy traffic, and it was the Sutton-bound downhill loop that retained the straight through track.
W E Robertson, ColourRail

Opposite bottom: No 9 at the Baily Post Office loop on its way to the Summit. This photograph was taken on 31 May 1959, the last day of operation. This scene brings me a great sadness. What a magnificent tram in such a lovely setting, and only hours before its demise. Just around the corner breath-taking views of Dublin Bay would enchant the traveller, looking down at the Baily lighthouse, King Griffin's fort, the Lionshead and the Candlesticks, well known rock formations projecting into the sea. How sad it is that it was all to cease so soon; nightfall would bring the final end. What lack of vision, what a tragedy it all was, as No 9 enacted the final part in a fatal drama. It brings me to tears.
W E Robertson, ColourRail

Above: No 7 has just passed the Baily View loop on its return downhill journey to Sutton. For a short run the tram travels along the public road with a central halt ('Convent Gate') to serve Stella Maris Convent. You will notice that at this point ascending trams crossed to the left hand (inland) side of the road. Elsewhere, the tram keeps to the right hand (seaward) side at all times, whilst ascending. This crossover necessitated passengers leaving the tram from the front platform when heading up hill, as there was no room on the inside of the track. The tram is about to cross over Carrickbrack Road which turned away from the stone convent wall and the tram will now enter Stella Maris reserve as far as the junction with Ceanchor Road.
CCQ 2165

Opposite top: Car No 2 has just descended the full length of reserve track from the Summit and is standing at the Baily View or Stella Maris loop. The lighted section lamp indicates that the tram from which the photograph was taken has just arrived from Stella Maris reserve and No 2 can now proceed forward. The conductor of No 2 will now switch off the light and clear the section ahead. Dick McGlue, the usual motorman on car No 2, was born in the dwelling to the left which was the original gate-keeper's house. Carrickbrack Road can be seen ahead. This loop favours neither direction, as both ascending and descending cars must swerve off course to enter the loop. The photo was taken on 2 October 1953.

W E Robertson, ColourRail

Opposite bottom: Two trams passing each other at the Summit end of the Baily View or Stella Maris loop. No 8, the ascending car, has been waiting at the section lamp for No 3 to descend before setting off up hill to the Summit halt. No 3 will continue until it reaches the centre of the loop where No 8 has already either deposited or collected passengers. One of the great joys of a tram ride was when cars passed on the loop. The gorse is in full bloom, so the shot was taken sometime in mid summer. The gentleman approaching the camera, between the trams, is not one of the tram crew and he is carrying what appears to be a saucepan of water. Perhaps he is about to have a cup of tea.

R L Ludgate

Above: Having ascended from Stella Maris loop, No 4 has just entered the Summit loop and will continue until it reaches the Balkhill end before coming to a halt. The section box just passed, is for cars going in the Sutton-bound downwards direction, to clear the track ahead as far as Stella Maris or Baily View loop. The young conifer trees to the right have long since reached full maturity and the main road has now been built along this section of the track. There is little evidence, facing in this direction today, that a tram ever climbed this hill. The Summit loop was one of the largest on the system with as many as five or six cars at a time arriving or leaving in peak summer traffic.

R L Ludgate

Opposite top: This is a splendid broadside view of No 6, having arrived at the Summit from Sutton. The Summit was possibly the best place to photograph the trams as the photographer had ample space to stand back and frame his shots. Many of the trams could be recognised from the side view. For example, car No 3 (on page 22) showed the distinctive hump or hog-backing of the waist and rocker panels, whereas on No 6 this was less pronounced. The humping was caused by excessive use of the hand brake in later years when the air brakes began to leak. The hand brake tended to pull the platforms down and cause the distortion.

R L Ludgate

Opposite bottom: This view, looking towards Howth, depicts Nos 6 and 4 passing at the Summit loop. The trams are well stocked with passengers and Mrs Ludgate, on the leading platform of No 4, poses for the photograph. Interested spectators stand or sit in the shelter of the waiting room and the timber building to the left is the parcels office. Originally, the company had a tram track running to the rear of the waiting room, behind the hedgerow, but this was seldom used and lifted in 1937. It now forms part of an avenue into the old battery house. Both the battery house and the waiting room are now private residences.
Toilets were provided by the company on the other side of the waiting rooms. They were identified as **fir** (men) and **mná** (women) and this was the only case were the Irish language was used officially in the entire Great Northern empire. The Summit halt had a general unkempt, rugged natural beauty about it.

R L Ludgate

Above: This time the view is looking back towards Sutton, with Sheilmartin Hill in the distant right. In the previous photograph the tram numbers were even, now they are odd. No 7 is heading back towards Sutton. The building on the left is Howth Summit Stores and is still there, marginally extended, but nonetheless quite recognisable and it still serves as a shop. The trams are almost completely empty and, apart from the man and boy on the rear platform of No 1, little is happening. It is probably evening time in this July 1958 scene and, by the amount of sweet wrappers and bags lying about, the Summit Store must have had a busy day. There are no signs of the tram crews. Some would say that they were having a pint on the Summit, but more likely they are in the saloon making out way-bills.

ColourRail

Opposite top: This is a rather rare study shot of motorman Peter Shiels changing the bullseye section lamp at Dungriffan loop, having returned from Howth station towards the Summit. The tram is No 7. If cars were travelling in convoy, then the leading car would change the signal and the others would travel in close proximity along the closed section. If two cars arrived and crossed at the loop simultaneously, neither man would alter the signal. If a signal lamp was on and no car arrived after a reasonable period, it was the conductor's duty to walk ahead and his car would follow after a suitable interval. The signalling system was fairly simple and failsafe and the procedures ensured that collisions were few.   *R L Ludgate*

Opposite bottom: No 3 is just passing Jim Bertie's cottage, having crossed over Balkill Road. Originally the Bertie family attended to the opening and closing of railway type gates at Balkill but, on account of sparse road traffic, this practice quickly fell into disuse. Instead, the tram would sound its gong continuously and edge forward slowly. This crossing was on a curve and relatively 'blind' so great caution had to be taken. It was also a set down stop for local passengers.The trolley pole was usually tied down from the Summit to Howth and the motorless gliding and clinking of the wheels against the tracks was delightful, especially when passing through 'Kruger's Cutting', when the sounds had a hollow resonance, giving a sense of breakneck speed, though this was hardly the case.   *Joe Pokorny*

Above: Every year various groups, societies and clubs, would hire out a tram or indeed, a few in convoy for a special outing or occasion. The Merrion Hall Sunday School excursion took place annually without fail and the members disembarked at Dungriffan halt making their way to the tennis grounds (now the GAA) for a pleasant evening, before returning to Howth station also by special arrangement. Recently, one of the members of this society came to the museum and boarded No 9 and yielded to a bout of tearful, happy, memories of days gone by. The Irish Railway Record Society often hired a car for tram enthusiasts and the London branch were also frequent visitors. This photograph depicts one such happy occasion, where No 10 has been hired out by the IRRS and carries their special plaque. The view is facing towards Howth and the unused gates at Balkill crossing are just visible behind No 7.   *Leeds transport Historical Society*

Opposite top: This tramless view in October 1953, shows the switch back at McGlue's Bank, facing towards the off shore islands. The tram tracks, or permanent way, had to be elevated well above the natural ground level and serpentined to spread out the severe gradient. The tram poles were normally on the seaward side, but on curves their position had to suit the draw of the overhead power cable. St Mary's national school is to the right, out of view, and directly ahead is the then recently constructed Grace O'Malley local authority housing development. There was a tradition in Howth of unofficially naming buildings or public works after a current event. For example, 'Somali village' was built when an exhibition in 1907 featured such a village 'on stilts' in Somalia and the local people felt these elevated houses merited the name. 'Kruger's Cutting', just a short distance away from this scene, honours the memory of a Boer War hero in the news at the time when the cutting was made and Grace O'Malley is known locally as 'Korea' as it was constructed during the Korean War of 1950-3.   *W E Robertson, ColourRail*

Opposite bottom: A very rare snowset view of car No 4 descending past a row of trees which run into Offington Wood. Thomas, the 3rd Earl of Howth, had two wives and his first wife, Lady Emily de Burgh, bore him a son and heir, William Ulick Tristram, and four daughters. One of these daughters, also called Emily, married Thomas Gaisford of Offington in 1859, exactly 100 years before the closure of the trams. The name 'Offington Wood' recorded this event. A local estate also bears the name.   *Joe Pokorny*

Above: Tram car No 8 is descending by Offington Wood with her trolley pole tied down. It was the practice during daylight hours, to run the trams by gravity from the Summit, as the fall was constant. This practice was to save the company the cost of the electricity, but at night time it was necessary that the trolley pole be engaged to provide lighting. Offington Woods formed the north-east boundary of Howth Estate and on passing by them, one knew that the final destination of Howth station was nigh. As one rounded the northern perimeter of the woods, the harbour and islands, which had been lost to view since the higher level, suddenly emerged in all their splendour and the refreshing smell of the sea was welcome indeed.

R L Ludgate

Opposite top: The trams were carried over two bridges or viaducts and the one shown here is over the main Howth to Dublin road as the tram enters Howth station. The contrast between the two viaducts could not be greater. The one at Stella Maris Convent is a fine impressive granite stone structure, with castellated top, brick arching and fine stepped stone buttresses. The tram, in passing over this viaduct, had a deep earthy sound. The Howth station viaduct was a steel girder structure with a considerable span and central supports carried on fluted columns with capitals. In the early days, the bridge had ornate sides, but when one of these panels fell away, it was decided, for reasons of safety, to remove them. When travelling over this viaduct, the sound dramatically changed to a reverberating hollow drone and you knew that you were floating at high level. This shot shows No 4 descending by gravity into the station. *R L Ludgate*

Opposite bottom: This is a lovely action shot of No 4 freely rolling down the viaduct incline into Howth station. The conductor has already commenced the time honoured practice of reversing the swivel backrests of the timber slatted seats for the return journey. The trolley poles of the Hill of Howth trams tended to be more distorted than with other systems and this resulted from the tying down. To prevent the trolley boom swinging violently from side to side, it was tied securely and this was wearing on both the trolley pole and the trolley stand springs, which can be seen to the left of the conductor. Howth railway station is in the background with its typical GNR yellow brick chimneys. *R L Ludgate*

Above: Of all the photographs in this book, this is one my favourites. No 7 stands at Howth station on a lovely summer day, casting a noon day shadow across the station wall. The tram is full of passengers and the conductor, out of view, has now pulled the trolley pole from the overhead cable wire and is about to re-appear around the side of the tram. They had to alternate the direction in which they walked to avoid over-winding and breaking the cable. The late John Hinde, a famous publisher of postcards, said that his most popular postcards all had a small splash of red which brought them to life. It was not unusual for him to plant a potted geranium on a windowsill to add this special touch. The bright red weighing machine, so popular before the arrival of the bathroom scales, adds just the perfect touch. How I would love to be on this tram, ready to set off into the shadows ahead! *R L Ludgate*

Opposite top: I love this photograph, taken in August 1956. It shows Billy Rankin, one of the most personable of the conductors, changing the trolley pole for the return journey to the Summit and Sutton. He pauses to have a little word with the two ladies busily engaged in conversation. The man in the trench coat and brown bag, slowly makes his way towards the tram. In the far off distance, to the left of the railway signal cabin, can be seen the Howth Lodge Hotel, known at the time as the Claremount. It commands a fine beach popular with travellers on the railway. The shelter, looking a little the worse for wear, is behind Billy. The overall atmosphere is one of relaxation and the absence of strife. They were good days.

C B C ColourRail

Opposite bottom: We now begin a survey of the Hill of Howth tram fleet. Our first three views were taken on the same day in October 1953. Here we see car No 1 traversing the stretch of track between Sutton station and Sutton Cross as it heads towards the Summit. The grass could do with a cutting! This car, in its latter years, was crewed by Tom Redmond, motorman, and Willy O'Brien, conductor. No 1 ran on the last day but, sadly, was not preserved. Mrs Redmond told me that she wept bitterly to see Tom's tram in a crumpled heap.

W E Robertson, ColourRail

Above: Car No 2, in the latter years, was manned by Dick McGlue and Des Farrell, although Dick was actually driving No 6 on the day of the closure as all crews had double shifts. Directly after the closure, an advertisement was placed in National newspapers seeking homes for all the trams and it was No 2 which was to find the furthest home away from home. She was taken by the Orange Trolley Museum at Perris in California, where she is now running once more. No 2 usually provided the early morning service and picked up a Mr Jameson, the great whiskey magnate, from his house in the Baily. Sometimes, Mr Jameson would hand a bottle of *Power's Whiskey* to Dick with the words, "Some more power for the tram, Dick". When No 2 was being cleaned out in Perris, several empty bottles of whiskey where found in the sand box – and, amazingly, one unopened!

W E Robertson, ColourRail

Opposite top: No 3 was the most loved of all the trams. Her crew, Bob O'Connor and Billy Rankin, were older than the rest and were renowned for their courtesy and politeness at all times. Customers would miss a tram especially to travel on No 3 as there was such a lovely and friendly atmosphere. Every Christmas, Bob and Billy would decorate No 3 with bunting, tinsel, bracts of holly and decorations. Some years a large Christmas tree was fitted to each end and bedecked with fairy lights and colourful baubles. They even had little gifts, nicely wrapped, for some of the regular customers. Some years, carol singers would adopt No 3 as their pitch and would sing their hymns to the rhythm of No 3's motors. On closure, No 3 was set aside for preservation at Guinness's Brewery, but was stripped so badly by souvenir hunters that, sadly, this most special of trams was eventually scraped. Here, she is seen at the Summit in October 1953.   *W E Robertson, ColourRail*

Opposite bottom: No 4 was special in that she was the tram that opened services on 17 June 1901. How splendid she must have looked, in her lovely livery of crimson lake and ivory, creeping her way through the gorse clad rocky outcrops and rugged maritime scenery of the Hill, with John Holland at the controls and Jack Graham collecting the first fare.The final crew of No 4 were Tom Whelan, motorman and Colm Weafer, conductor. On closure, No 4 was taken by the Belfast Transport Museum and placed on display in Witham Street. This museum is now part of the Ulster Folk and Transport Museum and is located at Cultra, a short journey from Belfast by train or bus and is well worth the visit. No 4 shares the company of Ireland's last horse tram, from Fintona, Co Tyrone, also in same blue and cream GNR livery. She is seen here on a busy day at Sutton.   *R L Ludgate*

Above: Car No 5 had a history of mishaps and misadventure. In 1912, Mary Waldron, the wife of the Summit gatekeeper, walked in front of No 5 and was tragically killed. Later, in the 1930s, a poor drunk wandered off course and collapsed in a sleeping heap in the path of the oncoming No 5. As it was dark he could not be seen on this section of reserved track. In both instances the company was found to be free of any responsibility for the accidents. In the summer of 1949, No 5 was in service around the Hill and had just arrived at the Summit halt when a thunder storm suddenly broke with a wild fury. The trolley pole was struck and the lightning travelled down the saturated trolley cord with such intensity that the upper deck surround was burnt in two and the whole front of the tram badly scorched. It is probably no surprise that No 5 was the first to be scrapped. Her last crew were Billy McNally, motorman and Pat O'Dowd, conductor.   *R L Ludgate*

Opposite top: If a fleet of trams could be described as a family, then No 6 would probably have been the shyest. None of the tram crews could recall any specific event associated with No 6. Her final crew was Bob Martin and John Montague. I met virtually all of the tram personnel over my many years of involvement with tram restoration, but I never met either Bob or John, though I do have a film showing John collecting fares on No 6. He was a slim, red-haired gentleman and I believe he became a conductor on the buses. On closure No 6, seen here at Sutton depot, was scrapped, but her bogies, control gear and running paraphernalia, were presented to the Manchester Museum of Transport and are now under a single-deck, open-ended tram. *C B C ColourRail*

Opposite bottom: No 7, seen here at Howth, was in her latter years operated by Peter Shiels, motorman and Jimmy Conlon, conductor. She was one of the spare trams, little used in the winter months when the system operated a skeleton service. Most of the standby motormen learnt to drive on No 7. There is a specific technique for bringing a tram to a halt in slippy, wet, conditions, when the friction between the brakes and rails is at a minimum. This was to apply the hand brake and tap the sand pedal in such a manner as to pepper the rails with dry, gritty sand. The sand provide the necessary friction to bring the tram to a halt. Beginners never quite got the art, with the result that the wheels jammed and then 'grinded' along the tracks, leading to 'flats'. After a while the worn ground-down section of wheel was favoured by braking, thus increasing the wear on steel tyres. No 7, the learners tram, became known as 'the tram with the square wheels' and had a clickety, clunk sound, more reminiscent of a steam locomotive. *L Ludgate*

Above: No 8 was crewed by Michael Fitzpatrick, motorman and Christy Brown, conductor. As was the case with No 7, No 8 was used chiefly in the summer months when a full service was warranted. In the early 1900s, when the renowned photographer, Robert Welch, came to Howth, he selected No 8 as his photographic model and followed her around the Hill taking photographs against the many changing backdrops for which Howth is so richly famous. Most of the postcards depicting trams, so popular in this era, showed No 8. Many of these postcards were painted and, of course, No 8 sported the earlier livery of crimson and white. In later years, when photography was within the reach of most families with the Kodak box camera, No 8 was rarely photographed. As a spare car, she was seldom out and, as with No 5, was scrapped two years before the final closure. I have film material of all the trams running but, sadly, none of No 8, the elusive tram. She is seen here descending into Howth past Offington Wood. *Leeds Transport Historical Society*

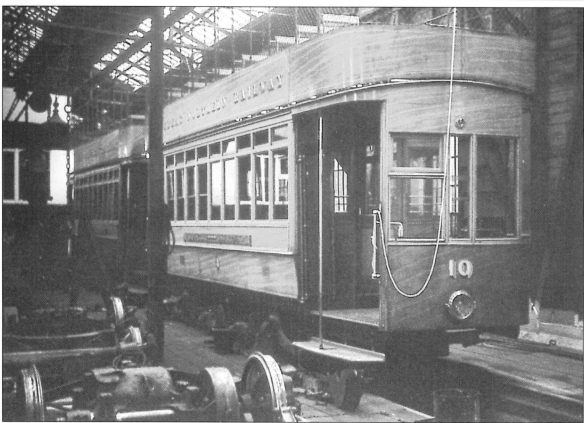

Opposite top: Tramcar No 9 has a special place in tram history in that she was selected to be the official last tram. On this auspicious occasion, she was operated by Christy Hanway, motorman and Alfie Reilly, conductor. Christy recalls the final run uphill towards the Summit halt, late on 31 May, a drizzly dank evening. As he trundled along with a heavy heart, the ever vigilant Christy noticed that all was not right with the track ahead as he approached Somali village. On bringing the tram to a complete halt, Christy and Alfie walked ahead to investigate and found that the tracks had been unbolted in part and to proceed could have caused a derailment. To the great disappointment of all the passengers and with an even heavier heart, Christy had to change platforms and commence the descent. The perpetrators of the deed were caught and brought to court by the Company. I was told by one of the individuals concerned that the prank was a wild effort to save the tram by drawing attention to its sad demise and prevent closure. Fortunately, no one was hurt. In this view the tram is seen at the Summit, in company with No 7. The lady crossing over the track to the left almost had a mishap   *CCQ 2166*

Opposite Bottom: The crew of No 10 was Jack Maypotter, motorman and Michael McGlue, conductor. Both Nos 9 and 10 were large, cumbersome trams and the bogies had an unusual wheel arrangement in that the driving wheels led, whereas usually the smaller pony wheels guided the heavy axle along. This arrangement had the serious disadvantage of being 'front heavy', more particularly on a downward run where there were steep corners, and the driving wheels would jump the track. For this reason, only the most careful and experienced motormen took the controls of Nos 9 and 10 and never descended to Howth station, where the most severe gradients and corners lurked in readiness for a derailment. When cars Nos 5 and 8 were scrapped in 1957, their 'cross-springs' were removed and fitted to Nos 9 and 10 and these prevented derailment. In 1958 these magnificent, but seldom used, cars gently eased their way into Howth station for the first time. I have a lovely piece of film of No 10 descending the switch-back at McGlue's bank. Happily, No 10 was presented to the National Tramway Museum at Crich in Derbyshire, where she was regauged and is now proudly on display. She is seen here inside Sutton depot.   *W E Robertson, ColourRail*

Left: No 11 was the works car and was seldom seen during daylight hours. It was often out at 5 am or 6 am on summer mornings to replace some section of overhead cable sorely in need of renewal. In the early days, the maintenance man was Paddy Kelly, who spent many years on top of his tower wagon, replacing, repairing and repainting. The tram had controllers at each end and access to the upper deck and tower was by ordinary ladders, bracketed to the sides. There was little regard for safety in those days with no guard rails on either the upper deck or tower platform and many a near-accident occurred. The worst Christy recalls was when he was up aloft on the tower, near the Baily lighthouse, very early one bright summer morning in 1940 during the Second World War. Suddenly, a floating mine struck the rocks just off the Baily, shattering the silence of the morning and almost toppling Christy from his high perch. "The tower swayed violently", said Christy, "and I clung to the pole for dear life."

R L Ludgate

Opposite top: The interiors of Nos 1-8 and Nos 9-10 were quite different and the contrast can be clearly seen in these two photographs. The former cars were built by Brush Electric of Loughborough, and ran on Brill 22E bogies. The longitudinal saloon seats, for 15 passengers each side, were timber-lathed and set back against the windows. In the 1930s, heating cylinders were located under the seats and cushions were fitted. The ceiling was known as a monitor roof, which is a form of concealed clerestory, and had small yellow ventilating windows which pivoted centrally on a horizontal line. Over the years the interiors darkened with age and constant varnishing, and the saloon creaked and strained as the tram swayed along. There were six windows to the side of the saloon and drop windows and sliding doors in the bulkheads separating the saloon from each platform. *R L Ludgate*

Opposite bottom: Nos 9-10 were designed as open-sided summer trams by the GNR drawing office in Dundalk and were built by G F Milnes and Co, Shropshire, on Peckham 14 D-5 bogies. The specification sought a monitor roof to match Nos 1-8, but the manufacturers provided a simpler, more modern roof style with hopper or fan light windows over nine large vertical openings. After a number of years it was decided to glaze the cars, as the fresh air of Howth was a little too fresh! The saloon seating arrangement resembled the upper deck of the old Dublin horse trams with central back to back, or knife board, seating creating an access aisle on each side. The purpose of this seating arrangement was to provide views for the passengers and avoid the original down-draught of an open-sided car. They served this purpose, but the side aisles were very tight and it was impossible for the conductor to collect fares without standing on toes. There were also fixed transverse seats at each end, providing for a total of 32 passengers. *R L Ludgate*

Above: Here we see Colm Weafer collecting fares on the top deck of No 4 as it passes over Howth viaduct on its way to the Summit. The upper deck arrangements of the two types of car were similar. Both had reversible garden seats on the upper deck. The larger trams, Nos 9 and 10, seated 41 (giving 73 including the saloon) whilst Nos 1-8 had 37 on the upper deck (total 67). The odd number of seats on the upper deck resulted from the fact that there was a single seat beside the trolley standard. Apart from No 2, the earlier cars had 'external' trolley pole springs as shown here, whereas Nos 2, 9 and 10 had 'internal' springs. The trolley standards had a splayed base on Nos 1-8, but there was a flat base, set on a levelling plank, on Nos 9 and 10. Otherwise the floor was cambered. Both types had high surround caging to protect passengers. The seats differed slightly. Nos 1-8 had wooden framing outside the back rest swivel support, whereas Nos 9 and 10 had a steel strip. *Joe Pokorny*

When No 2 arrived at Perris in California, it was immediately converted to the 4' 8½" gauge. After use for a short time, No 2 was abandoned outside and left there for many years. When I brought out my first book *Howth and her Trams*, I mentioned this fact and one evening, to my great surprise, I received a telephone call from Jim Fulton of Perris. He had read the book and said that it had spurred him into action. We immediately set up a friendship and over a period of years I sent all the information Jim sought and this was a very exciting period in my life. One year Jim visited me at Howth with film and photographs of No 2's progress. There we were – two Jims, both restoring Howth trams and we spent the long hours reminiscing about the glorious past and better days. I must confess to being small in stature but my name sake was a massive 6'5"!

David J Haynes

When restoration was complete Jim Fulton decided to make a postcard of No 2, reproduced here. He said that they had to wait weeks for an overcast sky to provide the right atmosphere. One could be forgiven for assuming that the view above was taken at Howth, though the absence of rugged hill scenery is obvious. Also obvious is the 'star spangled banner' adorning the leading end and the Irish Tricolour can be seen beyond. On occasions a lone piper plays solemn Irish airs on the upper deck as the passengers float nostalgically along. "It provides a touch of old Ireland," remarked Jim "and the Irish over here love it. It is our only open top tram and one of the most popular. We have St Patrick specials." So, happy to say, far from her rugged Irish hills, No 2 has a new lease of life.

Don Brown

Top left: Also preserved is No 4, now at the Ulster Folk and Transport Museum, Cultra, Northern Ireland. The tram restoration team and I have visited No 4 on many occasions and have sat inside her, soaking up past memories. She is seen here outside Sutton tram depot in April 1956. No 4 was the first tram to carry passengers on opening day, 17 June 1901, and survived to the bitter end.

ColourRail IR127

Top right: The complete undercarriage, controllers, resistors and running gear of No 6 were salvaged and bought by the Transport Museum at Heaton Park, in Manchester. They were regauged and refurbished and were placed under Manchester 'Californian type' single deck open ended tram No 765. In this October 1984 view we see Ellie Corcoran, daughter of our own museum's President, Michael Corcoran, wearing the motorman's hat.

M Corcoran

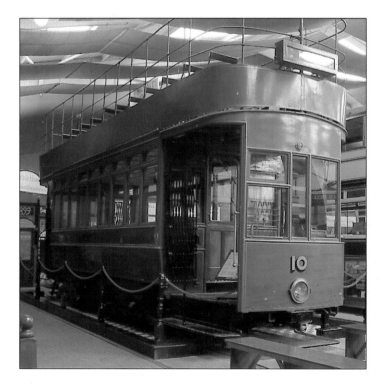

Bottom: No 10 was, without doubt, the most fortunate of the hill fleet. Directly after closure, she was taken by the National Tramway Museum at Crich in Derbyshire and regauged to 4'8½". She was kept at their Clay Cross depot for a number of years, awaiting full restoration. Our tram team visited her on several occasions, photographing her, measuring her and gathering information for the restoration of her sister, No 9, in Howth. No 10 is currently on display at Crich where she is seen in this August 1998 view.

W N Johnston

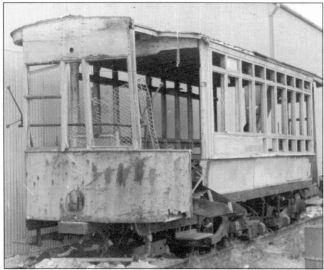

Top left: Unlike No 10, No 9 fell into a sad state, was vandalised beyond recognition and badly weathered. When I first discovered her in 1976, the upper deck was entirely gone, the bulkheads removed and the seating ripped out. No pane of glass survived. The worst sort of vandal is the 'enthusiast' or the souvenir hunter. Such a person stops at nothing to rip a carcass apart for the dubious honour of holding a keepsake. For these people, memories are not enough. They 'destroy' in their pursuit of trophies. Many honourable people returned their booty when they learnt about her restoration. Many have still to do so. *James Kilroy*

Top right: The tram restoration team at Howth. From the left: Brian Greene, John Kelleher, Bert Brown, Bob Dawson and myself. They are working here on No 224, a small open-front, open-top car, typical of turn of the century tram design. Missing from the picture are Brendan McGuire, Bill Garrioch and John Wheatly. *Larry Griffin, TMSI*

Bottom: No 9, now restored and seen returning from a St Patrick's day parade in 1991, watched by some admirers. Motors were obtained from Amsterdam and controllers from Denmark and all the running paraphenalia to power the tram is there, the power to put the heart and life back into No 9. However the cost of the heavy machinery involved is not there and so poor No 9 must wait until the funding is available to complete her restoration. How lovely it would be to see her run once again! *James Kilroy*